I HONESTLY CAN'T REMEMBER WHAT CATALYZED THIS DESIRE...
ZA (STEP)
...BUT FOR AS LONG AS I CAN RECALL, THERE'S SOMETHING I'VE ALWAYS ADMIRED.
SOMETHING I'VE DEVOTED MY WHOLE SELF TO BECOMING—
AN EMINENCE IN SHADOW.

Episode.1
Shadow 1
[Art]
Anri Sakano
[Original Story]
Daisuke Aizawa
[Character Design]
Touzai

THE
Eminence IN

[CONTENTS]

I Searched Everywhere for a Mythical Eight-Headed Serpent and Never Found It

PICTURE SOMEONE WHO ISN'T THE MAIN CHARACTER OR THE ANTAGO-NIST.
SOMEONE WHO MANIPULATES EVENTS BEHIND THE SCENES AND FLAUNTS THEIR OVER-WHELMING POWER.
THAT'S E KIND OF SHADOW-BROKER VE ALWAYS REAMED OF ECOMING.
MY REVERENCE FOR THEM WASN'T SOME SHORT-LIVED CHILDHOOD PHASE.
IT WAS SOMETHING THAT NEVER STOPPED DRIVING ME.
AT SCHOOL, I PLAYED THE ROLE OF A FOR-GETTABLE BACKGROUND CHARACTER...
...BUT BEHIND THAT FACADE, I WAS TRAINING FULL THROTTLE.

KARATE. BOXING. KENDO. MARTIAL ARTS.
I LEARNED ANYTHING AND EVERYTHING I COULD TO BECOME STRONGER, CONCEALING MY TRUE POWER ALL THE WHILE.
ALL SO THAT SOME-DAY...
...I COULD FINALLY BECOME A TRUE EMINENCE IN SHADOW!!
BUT WHEN I THOUGHT ABOUT IT...
...I REALIZED MY GOAL WAS IMPOS-SIBLE.
NO MATTER HOW STRONG I GOT, I'D NEVER BE ABLE TO TAKE DOWN AN ARMY.

AND IF SOMEONE DROPPED A NUKE ON ME, I'D GO POOF LIKE ANYTHING ELSE.
THERE WERE FIRM LIMITS ON HOW STRONG A LIVING CREATURE COULD GET.
HEADBAND: VICTORY
BUT THE SHADOW-BROKERS I DREAMED OF WOULD NEVER GET DONE IN BY A MERE NUKE.
SO I RACKED MY BRAIN.
WHAT COULD I DO TO NOT GET BLOWN TO BITS?
AND THAT'S WHEN I FOUND MY ANSWER...
RRY TTER

I HAD TO TURN TO THE UN-KNOWN.
I HAD TO LEARN MAGIC!!
HOWEVER, NO ONE ACTUALLY KNEW HOW TO DO THAT.
SO ALL I COULD DO WAS FOLLOW MY GUT.
I MEDITATED UNDER WATERFALLS. I FASTED. I CHANGED RELIGIONS.
I MASTERED YOGA. I CONTEM-PLATED REALITY.
I SEARCHED FOR SPIRITS. I PRAYED TO GOD. I CRUCIFIED MYSELF.
I STRIPPED NAKED AND SMASHED MY HEAD AGAINST TREES SO I COULD BECOME ONE WITH NATURE.
陰
LOINCLOTH: SHADOW

MY QUEST TO AWAKEN FANTASTIC POWERS CONTINUED, AND AT LAST, I SAW IT.
A BLURRY LIGHT.
I RAN TOWARD THE LIGHT, CERTAIN I'D FINALLY FOUND WHAT I WAS LOOKING FOR.
MAGICMAGICMAGICMAGIC
MAGICMAGICMAGICMAGIC
"HELL YEAH, IT'S MAGIC!!!"
PUAA (FLASH)

AND THAT WAS THE LAST THING I REMEMBER...

...FROM BEFORE I GOT REINCARNATED.

GAKIN (CLANG)

HYAH!

GIN (WHAM)

DOSA (SLUMP)
OW...
YOU'RE TOO STRONG, SIS...!

HYU (SWOOSH)
OH PLEASE, DON'T GO CRYING ON ME.
I MIGHT BE OLDER THAN YOU, BUT YOU SHOULD HAVE BEEN ABLE TO DODGE THAT.
CLAIRE KAGENOU (AGE TWELVE)
SIGH...
AND YOU CALL YOURSELF A KAGENOU...

KOOO (VWM)

WHEN YOU USE MAGIC TO STRENGTHEN YOUR SWORD AND BODY...

SUPAN (SLASH)

...YOU CAN SMASH BOULDERS JUST LIKE THAT.
WOOOOOW!!
GARA (CRUMBLE)
GARA

THAT WAS AWESOME! CAN YOU TEACH ME!?
KIRA (SPARKLE)
KIRA
THAT'S STILL A WAYS OFF FOR YOU.
AND BESIDES, IT'S GETTING LATE. THAT'S ALL FOR TODAY'S LESSON.

NOW, CLEAN UP THE RUBBLE.
ZA (TURN)
AWWW...

...
SIGH...

HEH HEH.

CID KAGENOU (AGE TEN)
※ THIS IS OUR PROTAGONIST.

I DID A DAMN FINE JOB PLAYING A WEAKLING TODAY, IF I DO SAY SO MYSELF.

I MEAN, I MASTERED USING MAGIC FOREVER AGO.

I DUNNO IF IT WAS THE TRAINING FROM MY LAST LIFE OR WHAT, BUT I'VE HAD ALL THAT STUFF FIGURED OUT SINCE I WAS A BABY.

HYOI (FWIP)
ひょい

HYOI
ひょい

YOU CAN USE MAGIC TO HEAL YOURSELF AND PERFORM INHUMAN FEATS OF STRENGTH.

IF I DID MORE TESTS, I BET I COULD DO EVEN COOLER STUFF WITH IT, BUT...

...A GOOD SHADOW-BROKER'S ALWAYS GOTTA MAINTAIN HIS COVER.

HEH...

OF COURSE, I'M STILL NOWHERE NEAR BEING ABLE TO BEAT A NUKE.

I FIGURED THAT'D BE FINE 'COS THIS WORLD DOESN'T HAVE CHEMICAL WEAPONS...

HYU (TOSS)

ヒュッ

BAGON (SMASH)

...BUT IT ISN'T!!!

WHAT GOOD IS A SHADOW-BROKER WHO SETTLES FOR LESS!!!?

BUNCHA MERCHANTS LUGGING LOADS OF FANCY ART THROUGH THE FOREST AT NIGHT...

GUESS NO ONE TOLD 'EM HOW SKETCHY THESE PARTS ARE.

DIDJA SEE THE WAY THAT OLD BAG LOOKED AT US WHEN SHE DIED!?

YEAH, SHE WAS BABBLING LIKE A DUMBASS AND BEGGING US TO SPARE HER SON.

SO I TOLD HER...

..."HAND OVER THE VALUABLES IF YOU WANT TO—"

GASHAN (CRASH)
!!?
HA HA !!!
BAAAAN (TA-DAA)
HEY, LOSERS !!!
HAND OVER THE VALUABLES IF YOU WANNA LIVE!!!
KATA (SHOCK)
WH...
WHAT'S UP WITH THE RUNT!?
※ THIS IS OUR PROTAGONIST.

I SAID HAND OVER THE CASH!!
YOU THERE, TRY JUMPING.
AH-HA! I HEARD A CLINK!
CHARIN (CLINK)
NO, SERIOUSLY, WHAT'S UP WITH THIS GUY!?
EASY THERE— SETTLE DOWN.
I'M JUST YOUR ORDINARY, RUN-OF-THE-MILL PIP-SQUEAK.

INGREDIENT: SLIMES

I HUNTED A BUNCH OF THEM AND MIXED THEM UP INTO JELLY FORM.

MIX AND PREPARE

THEN, I TOOK THAT JELLY...

...AND MADE IT INTO A FULL-BODY BODYSUIT AND A NIFTY LITTLE SWORD.

STRONG!

CHEAP!

AWE-SOME!

AND IT LOOKS BADASS, TO BOOT!

ORA ORA ORA ORA!!!
ZA (SLICE)
ZA
ZA
ZA
ORAAAAAAAAA!!!!
ZA
ZA
ZA

HAAA-HA-HA!
ORA ORA ORA ORA...
...ORA ORA ORA ORAAAA!
ZAKU
ZAKU
ZAKU (STAB)
※ THIS IS OUR PROTAGONIST.

SHIIN (SILENT)
...WAIT, HUH?

Y-YOU LITTLE ...
YOU WON'T GET AWAY WITH THIS ...
THERE'S ONLY ONE GUY LEFT?
WELP, GUESS YOU GET TO BE THE GUINEA PIG FOR HANDY-DANDY FEATURE NUMBER TWO.
BA (WSHH)
RUN YOUR MOUTH ALL YOU LIKE!!
I MIGHT NOT LOOK IT, BUT I'M A MASTER OF THE ROYAL BUSHIN METHOD!

UNDER-ESTIMATE ME, AND YOU'RE GONNA HAVE A BAD TIME!!
ZA (SLICE)
...HUH!?

DAMN YOU!
HYU (SWOOSH)
WHOA THERE.
HUH, SO THAT'S THE ROYAL BUSHIN METHOD?
HYUN
I HEAR IT'S ALL THE RAGE OVER IN THE CAPITAL THESE DAYS.
AND I GOTTA SAY, I'M A FAN OF HOW IT ISN'T ALL BOGGED DOWN BY TRADITION.
HYUN

DO
(WHAM)

SLIME SWORD, HANDY-DANDY FEATURE NUMBER TWO.
I CAN MAKE IT COME OUT WHEREVER I WANT, WHENEVER I WANT.
PROPS, MAN. YOU WERE STRONGER THAN MY SISTER.

GOSO (RUMMAGE)
GOSO

LOOKS LIKE THAT'S ABOUT IT... NOT A BAD HAUL.
THOSE BANDITS SURE WERE KEEPING BUSY.
DON'T YOU WORRY, MER-CHANTS.
I AVENGED YOU, AND YOU CAN REST EASY KNOWING YOUR CARGO WILL HELP FUND MY SHADOW-BROKER ACTIVI—
GATA (CLUNK)

...WHAT DO WE HAVE HERE?
A CAGE?
DID THEY HAVE A SLAVE ...?
PASA (RUSTLE)

HYUU
HYUU (WHEEZE)

IT'S A ROTTING CORPSE...

NO, WAIT. IT'S STILL ALIVE.

COULD THIS BE...

...ONE OF THE "POSSESSED"?

!

THIS WAVE-LENGTH... THIS IS FROM A MAGICAL OVER-LOAD!!

THAT MEANS THERE'S A HUGE AMOUNT OF MANA STORED INSIDE ITS BODY!!

PIRI (SHOCK)

JACKPOT!

IF THE CHURCH WAS JUST GONNA EXECUTE IT ANYWAY, THAT MEANS I CAN USE IT FOR MY MAGIC EXPERI-MENTS!!!

※ THIS IS OUR PROTAGONIST.

...OR SO I FIGURED, SO I RAN A BUNCH OF TESTS.

BUT MAN...

...I SURE WASN'T EXPECTING THIS.

SARA (SWAY)

WHO'DA THUNK THAT BLOB OF FLESH...
...WAS ACTUALLY A BLOND ELF.
NO WAY... MY BODY ROTTED SO MUCH, BUT NOW...
...IT'S BACK TO NORMAL!?
H-HOW CAN I POSSIBLY THANK YOU?
I PROMISE I'LL REPAY YOU, EVEN IF IT TAKES ME MY WHOLE LIFE...!!
NAH, DON'T WORRY ABOUT IT. THAT'S A LOT OF PRESSURE TO PUT ON A GUY...
WAIT, SHE WANTS TO SPEND HER WHOLE LIFE REPAYING ME...?
GASP!

SO BASICALLY, WHAT YOU'RE SAYING...
...IS THAT YOU WANT TO BECOME MY SHADOW-BROKER MINION?
HUH?
YEAH, THAT REACTION CHECKS OUT.
I ASKED HER TO BECOME MY MINION, BUT I DIDN'T EVEN EXPLAIN WHAT THAT MEANT.

GOING FORWARD, I GUESS I'LL NEED SOME SORT OF "OBJECTIVE."
SOMETHING THAT'LL REALLY HOOK HER IN...
?
?
......

ALL RIGHT, I'VE GOT IT.
FROM THIS DAY FORWARD, YOUR NAME WILL BE ALPHA.
YOU'LL BE MY FOLLOWER AND WORK ALONGSIDE ME.

OUR JOB...

...IS TO PREVENT THE RESURRECTION OF DIABLOS THE DEMON.

DIABLOS THE DEMON...?

THE ONE FROM THE FAIRY TALE?

EX-ACTLY.
"LONG, LONG AGO, DIABLOS THE DEMON PUSHED THE WORLD TO THE BRINK OF DESTRUCTION.
"BUT HE WAS DEFEATED BY THREE HEROES— A HUMAN, AN ELF, AND A THERIAN-THROPE." THAT'S HOW THE STORY GOES.
MOST PEOPLE DON'T KNOW THAT IT'S ALL TRUE.
AND THE STORY DOESN'T END THERE.
WITH HIS DYING BREATH, DIABLOS PUT A CURSE ON THE THREE HEROES.
HIS CURSE HAS BEEN PASSED DOWN THROUGH THEIR DESCENDANTS FOR GENERA-TIONS.

THE "CURSE OF DIA-BLOS."
GARI (SCRATCH)
がり
GARI
がり
IN OTHER WORDS, BEING POSSESSED IS PROOF THAT YOU'RE DESCENDED FROM ONE OF THE HEROES.
NO... THE "POS-SES-SION."
THAT'S WHAT WAS EATING AWAY AT YOUR BODY.
LONG AGO, SUCH PEOPLE WERE REVERED.
THAT... THAT CAN'T BE!
FORGET BEING REVERED, NOW THE POSSESSED ARE PERSE-CUTED!!
SOMEONE WENT IN AND REWROTE HISTORY.
THEY BURIED THE TRUTH AND ARE TRYING TO STAMP OUT THE HEROES' BLOODLINES.

THEY'RE CALLED THE CULT OF DIABLOS.

AND THEIR GOAL IS TO RESURRECT THEIR MASTER.

WE ARE THE SHADOW GARDEN.

WE LURK IN THE DARKNESS ...
...AND HUNT DOWN SHADOWS.

STOPPING DIABLOS'S REINCARNATION WON'T BE EASY.

BUT IF WE FAIL, THE WORLD WILL FALL INTO RUIN.

WILL YOU FIGHT WITH US?

I WON'T...

SO MANY PEOPLE JUST LIKE ME DIED WITHOUT EVER LEARNING THE TRUTH.

...LET THE CULT GET AWAY WITH IT ANY LONGER!!

NOW THAT I KNOW WHAT'S GOING ON...
...I'M READY TO DEVOTE MY LIFE TO THE SHADOW GARDEN.
THOSE EVIL-DOERS...
...MUST BE PUN-ISHED WITH DEATH!!
ZAA (CLENCH)
...NAILED IT.
THIS GIRL REALLY GOT INTO IT.
NEVER THOUGHT I'D GET SUCH A GENUINE REACTION OFF THAT IMPROVISED SETUP.
ZAAA

I MEAN, MOST OF THE STUFF I JUST SAID CAME OFF THE TOP OF MY HEAD.

IT'S NOT LIKE THE DEMON OR THE CULT OF DIABLOS ACTUALLY EXISTS.

end

The Eminence in Shadow

Episode.2

SINCE THE SHADOW GARDEN'S MOMENTOUS FOUNDING...
...ANOTHER THREE YEARS HAVE PASSED.

ALPHA AND I TURNED THIRTEEN YEARS OLD...
...AND MY SISTER CLAIRE, FIFTEEN.

ALL NOBLES GET SENT OFF TO A SCHOOL IN THE ROYAL CAPITAL WHEN THEY TURN FIFTEEN.
DOES MY SCHOOL UNIFORM LOOK GOOD ON ME?
SAY IT LOOKS GOOD. SAY IT.
OW, OW, OW.
AND MY SISTER WAS NO EXCEPTION, BUT...
BAN (SLAM)

...ON THE DAY SHE WAS SUPPOSED TO HEAD OUT...
...SHE GOT KIDNAPPED.
Episode 2

KA (GLEAM)
EVEN AT NIGHT, ABDUCTING CLAIRE IS NO EASY FEAT.
THE KIDNAPPER MUST BE SKILLED...
KAGENOU HOUSEHOLD DAD
SO...YOU'RE SAYING THERE'S NOTHING WE COULD HAVE DONE?
KAGENOU HOUSEHOLD MOM

HOW COULD YOU LET SOMETHING HAPPEN TO OUR FAMILY'S SOLE HOPE!
BAKI (SNAP)
バキ
BOKI (CRUNCH)
ボキ
I'M SORRY! I'M SORRY!!
WONDER IF I'LL END UP BALD TOO...

IN THIS WORLD, MAGIC LETS WOMEN BE POWERFUL TOO...
...SO IT'S NOT UNCOMMON TO HAVE FEMALE HEIRS INHERIT THE FAMILY NAME.
AS FOR ME, IT'S LIKE I'M NOT EVEN THERE.

THEY EXPECT NOTHING FROM ME, BUT THEY ALSO DON'T GIVE ME ANY ANNOYING RESPONSI-BILITIES.
I'M TOTALLY FORGETTABLE, AND I'VE WORKED HARD TO KEEP IT THAT WAY.
PATAN (CLICK)
パタ
WHEW...

YOU CAN COME OUT NOW...

...BETA.

KOTSU (STEP)

WHERE'S ALPHA?

SEARCHING FOR SIGNS OF MISS CLAIRE.

AS EXPECTED, THE PERPETRATOR IS A MEMBER OF THE CULT OF DIABLOS.

AND WHAT'S MORE, A HIGH-RANKING OFFICER.

ALPHA TAKES PEOPLE IN LIKE STRAY CATS, AND OUR RANKS HAVE SWELLED TO SEVEN NOW.

SO THIS IS A SLIME BODYSUIT...

THEY LOOK NICE, DON'T THEY?

ALL OF THEM PLAY ALONG WITH MY EMINENCE IN SHADOW CHARADE.

THEY PRETEND TO BELIEVE IN MY MADE-UP CULT TOO...

...AND LATELY, THEY'VE EVEN STARTED HELPING FLESH OUT THE PREMISE ON THEIR OWN.

THIS ANCIENT SCRIPT IS A SIGN OF THE CULT...

HYU (WHOOSH)

EVEN THOUGH THE CULT DOESN'T ACTUALLY EXIST...

KA (THUNK)

RIGHT THERE.

THAT'S WHERE THEY'RE KEEPING MY SISTER.

※ KNIFE HE THREW AT RANDOM

THEIR BASE TO THE NORTH IS A DECOY.
THE REAL ONE IS TO THE SOUTH.
HUH? BUT THAT AREA DOESN'T HAVE ANYTHING IN—

WAIT— IT CAN'T BE...!
BA (WSHH)
...!!
IF I COMPARE THIS TO THE DOCUMENTS...
※ KNIFE HE THREW AT RANDOM
...IT IMPLIES THERE'S A HIDDEN BASE IN AN UNDERGROUND FACILITY!

I CAN'T BELIEVE YOU LOOKED THROUGH ALL THOSE DOCUMENTS...
...AND SPOTTED THEIR HIDDEN MEANING IN THE BLINK OF AN EYE!!

YOU'RE A GENIUS, MASTER CID!!
BA
CALL ME SHADOW.
WE CARRY OUT THE RESCUE MISSION TONIGHT!
YES, MASTER SHADOW ...!!
AS YOU CAN SEE...
...NO MATTER WHAT NONSENSE I SPEW, THEY ALWAYS REPLY WITH OSCAR-WORTHY PERFOR-MANCES!
SOUTHERN UNDERGROUND FACILITY
KOTSU (STEP)
...CLAIRE KAGENOU.
HOW ARE YOU FEELING?

I HAVE QUITE A FEW THINGS I'D LIKE TO ASK YOU ABOUT.
JARA (RATTLE)
YOU LOOK FAMILIAR...
VISCOUNT... GREASE, WAS IT?
I'VE SEEN YOU AROUND THE CAPITAL.
YOU WERE IN THE BUSHIN FESTIVAL TOURNAMENT.
PRINCESS IRIS REALLY TORE YOU A NEW ONE.
VISCOUNT GREASE, THE FIRST-ROUND FLUNKER...

GA (SMASH)

PARA (CRUMBLE)
パラ
PARA
パラ

...ABLE TO DODGE THAT, WERE YOU?
I GUESS YOU'RE NOT LETTING YOUR STRONG MAGICAL POWERS OVERWHELM YOU.

I LEARNED FROM MY KID BROTHER THAT IT'S ALL ABOUT HOW YOU USE MAGIC, NOT HOW MUCH.
YOUR BROTH-ER...?

YEAH. HE'S A CHEEKY LITTLE BRAT.

EVEN THOUGH I ALWAYS WIN OUR FIGHTS...
...I'M CONSTANTLY LEARNING NEW THINGS FROM HIM.
THOUGH FOR SOME REASON, HE DOESN'T SEEM TO LEARN ANYTHING FROM ME...
THAT'S WHY I'M ALWAYS GIVING HIM SUCH A HARD TIME.

...ACTUALLY, SOMETHING LIKE THAT DID HAPPEN ABOUT A YEAR BACK.
BUT THEN ONE DAY, MY BROTHER ASKED ME TO DO SOME SORT OF "STRETCH"...
...AND FOR SOME REASON, I WAS ALL BETTER AFTER-WARD.

I SEE. SO YOU'RE SAYING YOU HAD SYMPTOMS.
THAT MEANS YOU MUST BE COMPATIBLE.
COM-PATIBLE ...?

NOTHING YOU NEED TO KNOW ABOUT.
BUT IT SEEMS I'LL HAVE TO LOOK INTO YOUR BROTHER AND SEE IF—
GO (SMASH)

IF YOU LAY A HAND ON MY BROTHER...

POTA (DRIP)

WHA...? YOU RIPPED THROUGH YOUR OWN FLESH!?

POTA

IF ANYTHING HAPPENS TO HIM...

...I'LL KILL YOUR FAMILY, YOUR FRIENDS, AND EVERYONE ELSE YOU—

...I'LL MAKE SURE YOU REGRET IT!!!

DOSA (SLUMP)

TCH... STUPID GIRL.

WELL, NO MATTER.

IF I EXAMINE THIS BLOOD, I CAN—

LORD GREASE!!

BANN (SLAM)

WE HAVE A PROBLEM!!

INTRUDERS IN THE MAIN HALL!!

DA (DASH)

WH-WHAT THE HELL...

...HAPPENED HERE!?

KO (TP)

BA (WSHH)

BYU (VOOM)
DOOOOO (KASHOOM)
WH-WHAT WAS THAT JUST NOW!?
NOT EVEN I COULD REACT TO THAT!!
SHII (DRIP)
WHO GOES THERE!?

WE ARE THE SHADOW GARDEN...
...AND OUR PURPOSE IS TO ELIMINATE THE CULT OF DIABLOS.
WE KNOW EVERY-THING.
KOTSU (STEP)
ABOUT DIABLOS THE DEMON, HIS CURSE...
...THE HEROES' DESCENDANTS... AND THE TRUTH ABOUT THE POSSESSED.
SU (POINT)
WHA...?
YOU PEOPLE...

ZAAA
(WHOOSH)
HOW DID YOU LEARN ...
...ABOUT THE CULT OF DIABLOS!!?

ONLY THE CULT'S TOP BRASS IS SUPPOSED TO KNOW ANY OF THAT!!
BA (WSHH)
IT COULDN'T HAVE BEEN LEAKED!!!
ZASHU (SLASH)
DO WATCH OUT.
...!?
GAKU (SLUMP)
WE WON'T KILL YOU YET.
KUSU (CHUCKLE)
KUSU
WE STILL HAVE OH SO MANY QUESTIONS FOR YOU.
SU (SWF)

KARI (CRUNCH)
PI (FLINCH)
BA (RIP)
HRAAAAAAH!
GO (SMASH)
OOOO (CRUMBLE)

WAS THAT A MAGICAL OVER-LOAD...?
HE'S GETTING AWAY. LET'S GO AFTER HIM!
THAT WON'T BE NECESSARY.
FUI (GRIN)
HE'S WAITING UP AHEAD.
HUH?
WAIT, YOU MEAN...
...HE KNEW THIS WOULD HAPPEN TOO?
HE TRULY IS A GENIUS...

BAN (BAM)
DAMN IT.
I'M LOST.
MAN, I DIDN'T KNOW THEY EVEN MADE BANDIT HIDEOUTS THIS BIG...
HUH?
KO (STP)
WHOA, WHO'S THIS GUY!?
HUFF... HUFF...
HE MUST BE THE BOSS OR SOME-THING!!!

HUH ...?

WHOA, THIS GUY'S PRETTY JACKED FOR A BANDIT.
HE'S GOT EVEN MORE MAGIC THAN ALPHA.
BIRI (TENSE)
BIRI

TOO BAD HE DOESN'T HAVE A CLUE HOW TO USE IT.
HE'S ONE OF THOSE MEATHEADS WHO THINKS THAT BUFFING HIMSELF UP IS THE END-ALL BE-ALL.
WHAT A WASTE OF PERFECTLY GOOD MAGIC.

SU (SLIDE)

GUESS IT'S ON ME...

GAKIN (CLICK)

...TO TEACH HIM HOW TO FIGHT MORE EFFICIENTLY.

YOU... SHEATHED YOUR SWORD ...!?

YOU'RE LOOKING DOWN ON ME!!

YOU LITTLE SHIT!!!

DA (DASH)

SUI (SHWP)

DO
(WHAM)
GO
(BA)
GO
∞
PARA
(CRUMBLE)
PARA
WH-WHAT WAS THAT!?
I SENSED ALMOST NO MAGIC, BUT THERE'S THIS MUCH POWER...!?
DAMN YOU!
DA

BAKII (SNAP)
...THIS DOESN'T MAKE SENSE.

HAVE... HAVE I EVER FELT THIS OUT-MATCHED BEFORE?
CERTAINLY NOT SINCE I WAS A CHILD.

IT'S THE SAME OVER-WHELMING GAP I FELT WHEN I SPARRED WITH MY TEACHER.

THAT SAME DESPAIR-INDUCING...
...DIFFERENCE IN RAW SKILL!!!

DAMN IT...
ANSWER ME.
GAKU (WOBBLE)
YOU PEOPLE APPEARED OUT OF NOWHERE.
JUST WHAT IS THE SHADOW GARDEN!!?

GUGU (TREMBLE)

IT DOESN'T MATTER ...

NO MATTER HOW STRONG YOU MAY BE, YOU'LL NEVER DEFEAT THEM!!

THE DARK-NESS OF THIS WORLD ...

...RUNS DEEPER THAN YOUR WILDEST DREAMS!!

THEN WE...
...SHALL DIVE DEEPER.
YOU DON'T KNOW WHAT YOU'RE TALKING ABOUT...
...KID!!!

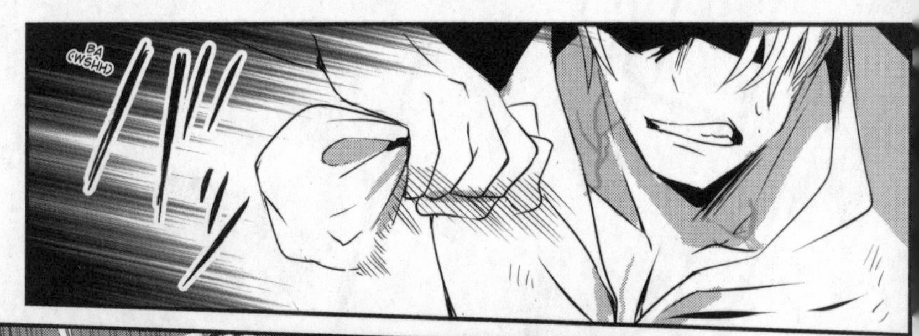

TAKING THESE PILLS...

...ALLOWS A PERSON TO SURPASS THEIR LIMITS...

GARI
(CRUNCH)

...AND BUILD UP TREMENDOUS AMOUNTS OF MAGIC IN THEIR BODY.

THIS IS THE POWER...

...OF "AWAKENING"!!!

AAA

AAAAAAAH!

DO
(WHAM)
BEKI
(SHUNK)
YOUR SWORD ...
ZU
(VRRP)
...WON'T WORK ON ME!!!
ZU

THIS IS STRENGTH!!
ZA (SLICE)
ZA
ZA
THIS IS POWER!!
ZA
YOU'RE SLOW!
YOU'RE WEAK!
YOU'RE SOFT!
ZA
ZA
ZA
THIS IS WHAT REALITY TASTES LIKE, KIDDO!!!
ZA

HUH...?
ZU (VRRP)
THE TIME FOR GAMES...
...IS OVER.
ZU
AH...
IT WASN'T JUST...

...AN OVER-WHELMING DIFFERENCE IN SKILL.

ZA (SLICE)

...MI...LLIA...?

MY SISTER'S HAND HEALED OVERNIGHT SOMEHOW, AND SHE HEADED OFF TO THE CAPITAL WITHOUT FURTHER ADO.

DUNNO WHY, BUT SHE STARTED MESSING WITH ME MORE THAN USUAL.

I GOTTA HAND IT TO THAT BANDIT GUY, THOUGH. HE PUT ON A GREAT SHOW.

FINDING A CHANCE TO USE THAT "THEN WE SHALL DIVE DEEPER" LINE WAS ON MY BUCKET LIST.

WHEN THEY TOLD ME ALL THAT, I WAS IMPRESSED BY HOW FAR THEY'D THOUGHT THE PREMISE THROUGH.

BUT THAT'S WHEN THEY SAID THEY WERE GOING TO SPREAD OUT ACROSS THE WORLD TO RESEARCH AND OBSTRUCT THE CULT.

I GUESS THAT WAS THEIR WAY OF SAYING THEY COULDN'T HANG OUT WITH ME SO MUCH ANYMORE.

HONESTLY, IT GOT ME FEELING A BIT SENTIMENTAL.

SO I SWORE TO THE SETTING SUN THAT I'D USE THAT AS A CHANCE TO GROW STRONGER...

...AND BECOME A REAL EMINENCE IN SHADOW.

end

THE
Eminence
IN
Shadow

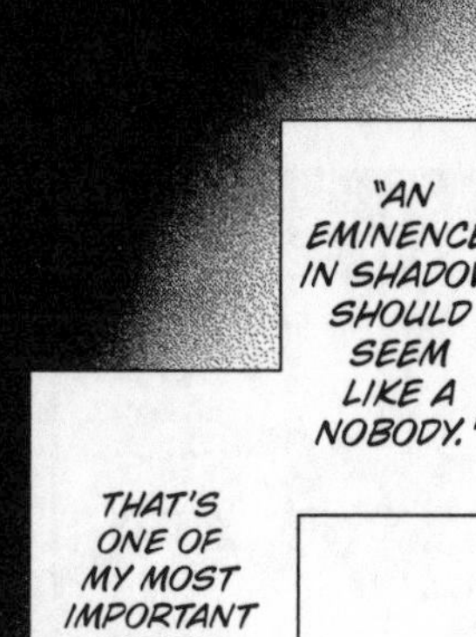

IN OTHER WORDS, BEING AN EMINENCE IN SHADOW AND BEING A NOBODY ARE TWO SIDES OF THE SAME COIN.

AFTER ALL, THEY'RE CALLED THAT BECAUSE THEY WORK FROM THE SHADOWS.

SO IF I STOOD OUT, I'D JUST BE AN EMINENCE.

Episode.3

Episode.3

AND THAT'S ...

...JUST AS TRUE HERE AT THE ACADEMY!!

THIS IS THE MIDGAR ACADEMY FOR DARK KNIGHTS IN THE ROYAL CAPITAL.
ZAWA (MURMUR)
ZAWA
IT'S THE FINEST SCHOOL ON THE CONTINENT, AND PROMISING YOUNG NOBLES GATHER HERE FROM ALL OVER.
ONCE I FINALLY TURNED FIFTEEN, I ENROLLED, JUST LIKE MY SISTER.
IN THE TWO MONTHS I'VE BEEN HERE, I'VE KEPT MY GRADES JUST UNDER AVERAGE...
...AND AM BLENDING PERFECTLY INTO THE CROWD.
HEYA, CID!!

THOSE THE RESULTS FROM THE PRACTICAL EXAM!?
WHAT'D YOU GET? WE BOTH GOT Bs.
SECOND SON OF BARON ETAL SKEL
SECOND SON OF BARON TATO PO

OH, I GOT A C.
IT SAYS I DON'T HAVE ENOUGH MAGIC.
FOR REAL!? WELL...
...YOU REMEMBER THE BET WE MADE, DON'T YOU?

WHOEVER DOES THE WORST ON THE TEST...
...HAS TO DO A DARE!!

SORRY...

...BUT I'M NOT INTER-ESTED.

KIPPARI (BLUNT)

BUT THAT'S THE SCHOOL IDOL FOR YOU.
PRINCESS ALEXIA MIDGAR.
IT'S LIKE SHE'S SAYING THAT CHILDISH FLINGS ARE BENEATH HER...

WHO-EVER DOES WORST ON THE TEST HAS TO ASK A GIRL OUT!!
THAT WAS THE BET!!

Y-YEAH, BUT...IT'S EMBAR-RASSING, AND SHE'S JUST GONNA REJECT ME.
DUH. THAT'S WHAT MAKES IT FUNNY.

I WANNA SEE HOW PATHETIC YOU LOOK AFTER GETTING BRUTALLY SHUT DOWN.
YOU'RE THE SCUM OF THE EARTH.

GO GET 'ER, CHAMP!!
DON'T WORRY, IT'S NOT LIKE YOU HAVE ANY SHOT AT ALL!!
TA (DASH)
DAMN IT ALL...
I'LL GET YOU TWO BACK FOR THIS, MARK MY WORDS!!

...AS IF!
FU (SMIRK)
I'VE BEEN WAITING FOR THIS DAY FOR AGES!!

HEADBAND: VICTORY

P—

P—

P...

PWIN-SHESH ALEXIA...

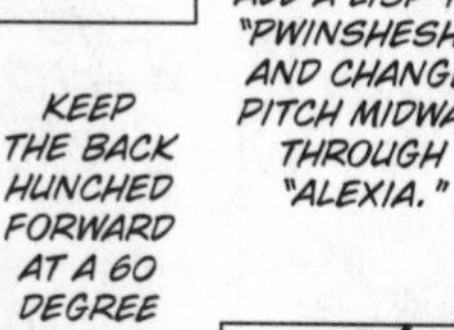

THEN, WITHOUT A MOMENT'S DELAY, RAISE YOUR RIGHT HAND AND HOLD IT THERE.
BUN (WHOOSH)
THE KEY HERE IS THE DISTANCE BETWEEN THE TWO OF YOU.
THE OPTIMAL GAP IS A SLIGHTLY DISTANT SEVENTY-TWO INCHES.
72
FROM THERE, DROP AS FAST AS YOU CAN...
BA (WSHH)
...TO A HARD RIGHT ANGLE!!!!
P-P-PLEASE ...
BISHI (SNAP)
...GO OUT WISH ME...?
90

...THAT WAS PERFECT.
I NAILED IT...!!
MY LINES CAME OUT LAME...
...AND THE QUESTION MARK I STUCK AT THE END MADE ME COME OFF TOTALLY INSECURE.
NOW THIS IS WHAT A BACKGROUND CHARACTER LOOKS LIKE.
IT WAS ALMOST A WORK OF ART.
I'M SATISFIED WITH MY PERFORMANCE!! EVERYTHING WENT JUST RIGHT!!
90
......

OH MY, I'M THRILLED.
I LOOK FORWARD TO OUR TIME TOGETHER.
GYU (SQUEEZE)
ぎゅっ
HUH?

SORRY... WHAT WAS THAT?

UH...

UM...

PA (JUMP)

ぱっ

?

I SAID, I LOOK FORWARD TO IT.

YOU WANTED TO GO OUT WITH ME, DIDN'T YOU?

WH—

WH—

※STACCATO

WHEN THE HELL DID I TURN INTO A ROMCOM PROTAGO-NIIIIIIST!!?

※VIBRATO

IT'S WEIRD, RIGHT?
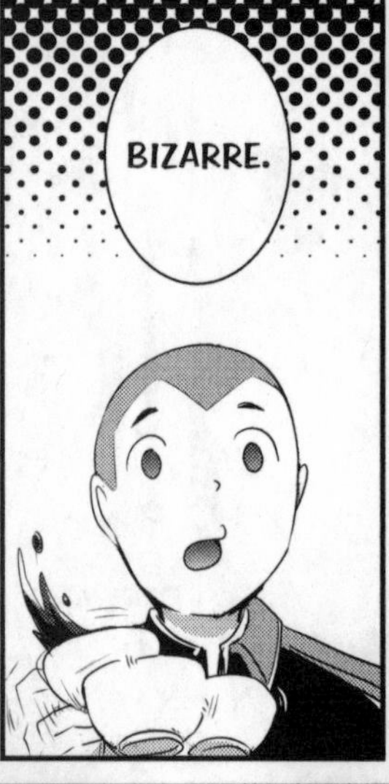
BIZARRE.

TOTALLY BONKERS.

WHY WOULD SHE GIVE THAT DUKE'S SON THE COLD SHOULDER...
...THEN TURN AROUND AND AGREE TO GO OUT WITH SOMEONE LIKE ME!? IT DOESN'T ADD UP!
ZAWA (MURMUR)
ZAWA
HEY, BE HAPPY. DON'T LOOK A GIFT HORSE IN THE MOUTH.

I GUESS A PRINCESS LIKE HER'S GOTTA BE BORED WITH STUDS LIKE ME...
...SO SHE WENT FOR SOMEONE A LITTLE LAMER.
BURU (QUIVER)
BURU
GIRI (GRIND)
GIRI
YOU CAN AT LEAST HIDE YOUR FEELINGS A BIT, MAN.

HISO (WHISPER)
HEY LOOK, THAT GUY'S THE PRINCESS'S BOYFRIEND.
BUT HE LOOKS SO AVERAGE!
HISO
I HEAR HE BLACK-MAILED HER INTO IT.
HISO
HE'S DEAD MEAT...

SHIT. I'M STANDING OUT.

AT THIS RATE, EVEN IF I GET A CHANCE TO SHOW OFF MY TRUE POWERS...
...I WON'T BE ABLE TO CALL MYSELF AN EMINENCE IN SHADOW!!
I'VE GOTTA DO SOMETHING ABOUT THIS...AND FAST!!

NOBODY CAN KNOW I ASKED HER OUT ON A DARE...CAN I COUNT ON YOU?
OF COURSE, MAN.
I SWEAR ON OUR FRIENDSHIP, I WON'T SAY A WORD!!

WHAT ARE YOU ALL TALKING ABOUT?
KOTSU (STEP)
PRINCESS ALEXIA!!

DO YOU MIND IF I DINE WITH YOU?
P-P-PWEASE DO!
IF YOU'D HAVE US!
KACHA (CLACK)
KACHA

WOW. I NEVER REALIZED...

...THE FILTHY-RICH LUNCH COURSE HAD SO MUCH FOOD.

I KNOW. I CAN NEVER EVEN FINISH IT.

HONESTLY, I'D BE HAPPIER WITH ONE OF THE CHEAPER ONES...

...BUT IF I DON'T ORDER THIS, OTHER PEOPLE WILL FEEL AWKWARD BUYING IT.

SU (SLIDE)
OH, THEN YOU WON'T MIND...
...IF I SNAG YOUR ENTRÉE.

HEE HEE...
I SEE YOU HAVE A BIG APPETITE.
EAT AS MUCH AS YOU LIKE.
HAVE SOME BREAD TOO.

SAY...
...YOU HAVE ROYAL BUSHIN FOR YOUR PRACTICAL ELECTIVE IN THE AFTERNOON, RIGHT?
SO DO I. LET'S TAKE IT TOGETHER.

I PULLED SOME STRINGS TO GET YOU INTO THE TOP-RANKED SECTION WITH ME.
CONSIDER IT A ROYAL ORDER.

HUH... SO THIS IS THE TOP-RANKED CLASS.
THE FACILITIES AND LESSONS HERE ARE DEFINITELY WAY NICER.
ZAWA (MURMUR)
ZAWA
ザワ
ザワ

THE ROYAL BUSHIN LESSONS ARE SEPA-RATED INTO DIFFERENT CLASSES BY SKILL.
BECAUSE I ONLY JUST ENROLLED, I WAS STILL IN THE LOWEST RANK.
THE UNIFORMS FOR EACH SKILL LEVEL ARE DIFFERENT TOO.
TOP RANK IS BLACK, BOTTOM RANK IS WHITE.

PAN (CLAP)
パン
PAN
パン
ALL RIGHT, EVERY-ONE!
TAKE FIVE AND GATHER UP OVER HERE.

STARTING TODAY, CID KAGENOU WILL BE JOINING OUR CLASS.
LET'S MAKE SURE HE FEELS WELCOME!

BUT MR. ZENON, HE'S A WHITE ROBE.
HE'LL JUST GET IN THE WAY.
COME ON NOW, I TOLD YOU TO MAKE HIM FEEL WELCOME.
NIKO (SMILE)
AND BESIDES, HE COMES RECOMMENDED BY PRINCESS ALEXIA.

WELL, IF THE PRINCESS IS ALL RIGHT WITH IT...
WELL, IF MR. ZENON'S ALL RIGHT WITH IT...
LOOKS LIKE THE PRINCESS IS PRETTY POPULAR...
KOTSU (STEP)

SORRY TO KEEP YOU WAITING, CID.
LET'S GO AHEAD AND HAVE A SPAR.
SPAR? WITH YOU? SCREW THAT, YOU'LL CRUSH ME.
DON'T WORRY. I'LL MAKE SURE TO HOLD BACK.
GEE, THANKS.
SIGH.

HER MOVEMENTS ARE REFINED.
...GUESS THAT'S A PRINCESS FOR YOU.
THIS IS SOME POLISHED, EFFICIENT SWORDPLAY.
SHE'S CLEARLY PUT A LOT OF WORK INTO PERFECTING THE BASICS.

HER OLDER SISTER PRINCESS IRIS IS SUPPOSED TO BE A GENIUS AND THE STRONGEST SWORDSWOMAN IN THE NATION...
...BUT IT LOOKS LIKE ALEXIA WENT THE OPPOSITE WAY AND GOT HER SKILLS THROUGH RAW EFFORT.

...
YOUR SWORD WORK.
IT'S NOT BAD.

MY APOLOGIES. I DIDN'T MEAN TO HIT IT THAT HARD.

IT'S FINE. DON'T WORRY ABOUT IT.

THAT WAS DEFI-NITELY ON PUR-POSE.

カラン KARAN (CLATTER) カラン KARAN

YOU NEED TO BE MORE CAREFUL, ALEXIA.

スッ SU (SWF)

MR. ZENON ...!!

TOP-RANK CLASS ADVISER ZENON GRIFFEY

HERE YOU GO, CID.
YOU'VE GOT QUITE A KNACK FOR THIS. I WOULDN'T HAVE THOUGHT YOU WERE A FRESHMAN.
THANKS.
AS YOU KNOW, THE ROYAL BUSHIN METHOD...
...IS AN INNOVATIVE OFFSHOOT FROM THE MORE TRADITIONAL BUSHIN METHOD.
THERE WAS SOME PUSHBACK AGAINST IT AT FIRST...
...SO I'M GLAD THERE ARE SO MANY YOUNGSTERS LIKE YOU PICKING IT UP NOW.
IT'S AN HONOR TO MEET YOU, SIR.
I KNOW YOU'RE ONE OF THE PEOPLE WHO HELPED POPULARIZE IT.
PLEASE, YOU'RE MAKING ME BLUSH.
PAAAA (SHINE)
COMPARED TO PRINCESS IRIS, I BARELY DID ANYTHING.

WE'RE MADLY IN LOVE, YOU SEE.

WOULD YOU MIND NOT GETTING BETWEEN US?

PETO (SQUEEZE)

...
YOU CAN'T KEEP RUNNING FOREVER.
I'M JUST A KID. GROWN-UP STUFF IS TOO MUCH FOR ME.

HE'S NOT MY FIANCÉ, JUST A SUITOR.

AND YET HE KEEPS TRYING TO MOVE THINGS FORWARD LIKE IT'S A DONE DEAL. IT'S REALLY QUITE A PAIN.

DON'T GO GETTING ME WRAPPED UP IN YOU TWO'S NONSENSE!

YOU ONLY ACCEPTED MY CONFESSION BECAUSE YOU WANTED SOMEONE HARMLESS, RIGHT?

HOW CRUEL OF YOU TO TOY WITH MY TENDER MALE HEART!

OH?

DOESN'T THAT GO FOR BOTH OF US?
MR. I-ASKED-A-GIRL-OUT-ON-A-DARE, CID KAGENOU.
NIKOO (GRIN)
D— D—
※STACCATO
GO (MENACING) GO GO
D-DARE?
GO
I HAVE NO IDEA WHAT YOU'RE TALKING ABOUT.
GO GO
YOUR FRIEND... PO, WAS IT?
GO

WHEN I WENT TO HAVE A CHAT WITH HIM, HE BLABBED ALL SORTS OF THINGS I DIDN'T EVEN ASK ABOUT.
YOU'RE LYING! PO WOULD NEVER BETRAY ME LIKE THAT! THAT BASTARD, I'M GONNA MAKE HIM INTO MASHED POTATOES!
I DON'T THINK YOU MEANT TO SAY THAT LAST BIT OUT LOUD.
HOW HORRIBLE... TOYING WITH A YOUNG MAIDEN'S HEART...
SHIKU (SOB)
SHIKU
WHEN PEOPLE FIND OUT YOU MADE A PRINCESS CRY, THEY'LL HAVE YOU IN THE GALLOWS IN NO TIME...
DAMN IT, THIS PRIN-CESS...
...IS JUST A MONSTER IN DISGUISE!!!

FINE. I'D RATHER NOT BE EXECUTED.
I'LL PLAY ALONG. FOR NOW.

BUT I'M JUST THE SON OF A MINOR BARON.
I'M NOT ENOUGH TO STOP HIM.
AND BESIDES, WHAT'S WRONG WITH MR. ZENON?
GOSO (RUSTLE)

YOU SAW IT TOO, DIDN'T YOU? THAT SHADY SMILE OF HIS.
HE MAY BE HOT, SUCCESSFUL, RENOWNED, POPULAR, AND A TOP-SHELF SPECIMEN ALL AROUND...
...BUT HERE'S THE THING.

PERFECT PEOPLE DON'T EXIST.
CHARIN (CLINK)
ANYONE WHO CLAIMS TO BE IS EITHER LYING OR MESSED UP IN THE HEAD.
CHARIN
COMPARED TO THAT...
...I'D MUCH RATHER DEAL WITH AN EASY-TO-READ SCUMBAG LIKE YOU.

YES.

ZA (SCOOP)

ZA

YOU'D BETTER BELIEVE IT.

ZA

GOOD BOY.

NOW, YOU TOOK THE MONEY, SO I EXPECT YOU TO DO WHATEVER I—

ZA

ZA

ZA

ZA

ZA

ZA

GUI (YANK)

LISTEN TO ME!

WE'RE GOING TO KEEP PRETENDING TO BE LOVERS...
...FOR AS LONG AS IT TAKES TO MAKE THAT MAN GIVE UP.
DO I MAKE MYSELF CLEAR...
...FIDO? ♡

BUN (WHOOSH)

LOOK, FIDO — A COIN! GO FETCH!

AND THAT'S HOW I ENDED UP IN A FAKE RELATIONSHIP WITH A PIECE-OF-SHIT PRINCESS.

TA (DASH)

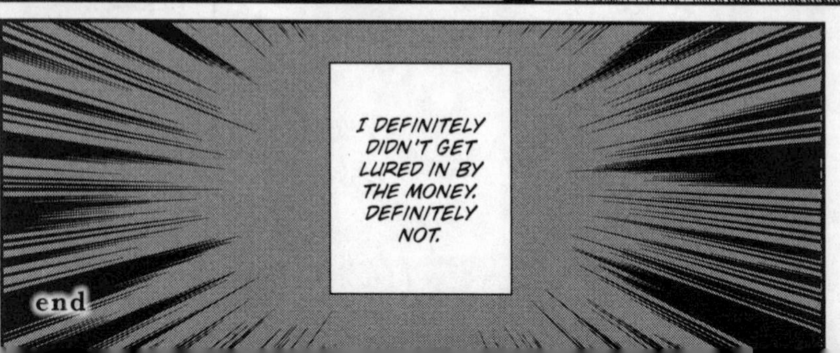

The Eminence in Shadow

Episode.4

IT'S BEEN TWO WEEKS SINCE I STARTED MY (FAKE) RELATION-SHIP WITH ALEXIA...
...AND WE'VE TAKEN TO TRAINING TOGETHER AFTER SCHOOL.

ALEXIA USUALLY PUTS UP A SICKEN-INGLY FAKE FACADE...
...BUT AROUND ME, SHE STARTED BEING HERSELF MORE.
AND AS WE SPENT MORE TIME TOGETHER...

...I GRAD-UALLY REAL-IZED...
...THAT I ACTUALLY REALLY...

...DIDN'T LIKE HER ONE BIT.
YOU WERE THE ONE WHO DOODLED ON MY UNIFORM, WEREN'T YOU?
HEE!
YOU LOOK GREAT, FIDO! ♡
HEE!
GO (MENACING)
GO
GO
GO
YOU KNOW, FIDO, I'M FEELING A LITTLE PARCHED.
WOULD YOU BE A DEAR AND GET ME SOMETHING TO DRINK?
WHAT AM I, YOUR SERVANT?
GET YOUR OWN DAMN DRINKS!

Episode 4

C'MON, FETCH!
CHARIN (CLINK)
CHARIN
SHUPA (ZOOM)
YOUR MINERAL WATER, MA'AM.

THAT'S WHY I CAN'T STAND HIM.
HE THINKS HE'S INVINCIBLE JUST BECAUSE HE'S DECENT WITH A SWORD.

I MEAN, HE'S GOOD, SURE...
HYU (WHOOSH)
KA (CLANG)
...BUT AREN'T YOU ABOUT AS STRONG AS HIM?
KAN

...A WHITE ROBE LIKE YOU MIGHT NOT BE ABLE TO TELL.
KIN (CLING)
KAN
I'VE PUT IN LOADS OF HARD WORK...
...AND EVEN I CAN TELL HOW STRONG I'VE GOTTEN.

BUT THAT DOESN'T CHANGE THE FACT...THAT I HAVE NO TALENT.
PEOPLE EVEN CALL MY SWORD WORK "MEDIOCRE."

I'VE SPENT MY LIFE BEING COMPARED TO MY GENIUS SISTER IRIS...
...SO I KNOW JUST HOW LARGE THE GAP BETWEEN "GENIUS" AND "MEDIOCRE" IS.

BUT ONE DAY, MY SISTER TOLD ME SOMETHING.

"I LIKE YOUR SWORDPLAY," SHE SAID.
IT FELT AWFUL. LIKE SHE WAS MAKING FUN OF ME.

EVER SINCE THEN...
KIN (CLANG)
...I'VE HATED THE WAY I FIGHT.

WHAT WAS THAT...
...ABOUT MEDIOCRE SWORD WORK?

N-NO WAY! IT BROKE!?
EVEN THOUGH IT WAS JUST A PRACTICE SWORD, IT STILL SHOULD HAVE BEEN PRETTY STURDY...
HOW DID YOU—?
YOU'RE RIGHT. I'M TOTALLY MEDIOCRE.

BUT I...
...HAVE SOMETHING I NEED TO ACHIEVE, NO MATTER WHAT.
KOTSU (STEP)
SO I'VE WORKED TOWARD IT...

...ONE STEP...
...AFTER ANOTHER.
NEVER STOPPING.

THAT'S WHY I CAN TELL JUST HOW MUCH WORK YOU'VE PUT IN.

I LIKE YOUR SWORDPLAY.

BECAUSE IT'S MEDIOCRE, LIKE MINE.

LOOKS LIKE I GOT LUCKY WITH WHERE I HIT YOUR SWORD OR SOMETHING.

NOW WHAT TO DO ABOUT THIS? I WONDER IF MR. ZENON WILL GET MAD...

...

KOTSU

FIGURE IT OUT YOURSELF.

I'M GOING TO HEAD BACK ALONE TODAY...

WAI
(CHATTER)
ワイ
WAI
ワイ

WOW, FEELS LIKE IT'S BEEN FOREVER SINCE ALL THREE OF US ATE TOGETHER.

KE
(LEER)
ケッ
YEAH, 'COS CID'S BEEN EATING WITH THE PRINCESS EVERY DAY.

I DON'T FEEL LIKE HANGING OUT WITH A TRAITOR.
LOOK, I SAID I WAS SORRY FOR TELLING HER ABOUT THE DARE.
I EVEN SHAVED MY HEAD AS AN APOLOGY.
IT WAS LIKE THAT TO BEGIN WITH.

DO YOU HAVE A MINUTE?

MR. ZENON!

WHAT IS IT?

...DON'T PANIC, BUT THERE'S SOMETHING YOU SHOULD KNOW.

ALL THEY FOUND WAS ONE OF HER SHOES ON THE WOODED PATH NEAR THE SCHOOL...

...AND SIGNS OF A STRUGGLE NEARBY.

THEY'RE TREATING IT... AS A SUSPECTED KIDNAPPING.

WH...WHAAAAAT!?

GATA (CLATTER)

HOW COULD THIS HAPPEN TO THAT HEARTLESS LITTLE—

UH, I MEAN...

—TO MY PRECIOUS GIRLFRIEND!!?

WE WERE TOGETHER UNTIL AFTER SCHOOL YESTERDAY.

DOES THIS MEAN THEY KIDNAPPED HER RIGHT AFTER THAT!?

THAT'S RIGHT...

THE KNIGHT ORDER WOULD LIKE TO HAVE A WORD WITH YOU.

ZA (STEP)

I ASSUME YOU'LL COME QUIETLY... RIGHT?

GASHI (GRAB)

...I SEE.
THANK YOU FOR YOUR REPORT.
IT REALLY DOES SEEM LIKE THIS STUDENT, CID KAGENOU...
...IS THE MOST SUSPICIOUS, DOESN'T IT, MARQUESS ZENON?
PRINCESS IRIS MIDGAR
ALEXIA'S OLDER SISTER

THAT'S RIGHT... MOST ARE IN AGREEMENT ON THAT.
BUT AS AN INSTRUCTOR, I HAVE TO SAY...
...HIS SWORDPLAY IS THE EPITOME OF MEDIOCRITY.

PLEASE, I'M BEGGING YOU...
...LET MY BROTHER GO!!

C-CLAIRE! WHAT ARE YOU DOING!? THAT'S A PRINCESS YOU'RE TALKING TO!
...AND YOU ARE?

I'M CLAIRE KAGE-NOU...
...CID KAGENOU'S SISTER!!

SHE'S AN ACADEMY STUDENT WITH EX-CEPTIONAL MARKS...
...AS WELL AS A PROVISIONAL MEMBER OF THE KNIGHT ORDER.
WELL, WE CAN AT LEAST HEAR HER OUT.

I HEARD MY BROTHER IS...THAT YOU'VE BEEN TORTURING CID FOR THE PAST FIVE DAYS STRAIGHT!
BUT HE'S INNOCENT— I KNOW HE IS!!
TORTURING? I WOULD HOPE NOT.

THE KNIGHT ORDER IS SIMPLY TAKING EVERY PRECAUTION TO AVOID ANY MISTAKES.
IT HASN'T BEEN CONFIRMED THAT YOUR BROTHER IS THE CRIMINAL.

BUT IF NO ONE FINDS THE REAL CULPRIT, MY BROTHER'S THE ONE WHO WILL TAKE THE FALL!!
HE'D NEVER DO SOMETHING HORRIBLE LIKE KIDNAP SOMEONE!!
MY BROTHER WOULD NEVER HURT A FLY!!

ALEXIA...

...PLEASE BE OKAY...

I CAME BACK WHEN BETA GOT IN TOUCH WITH ME.

IT LOOKS LIKE THIS HAS BECOME QUITE A MESS.

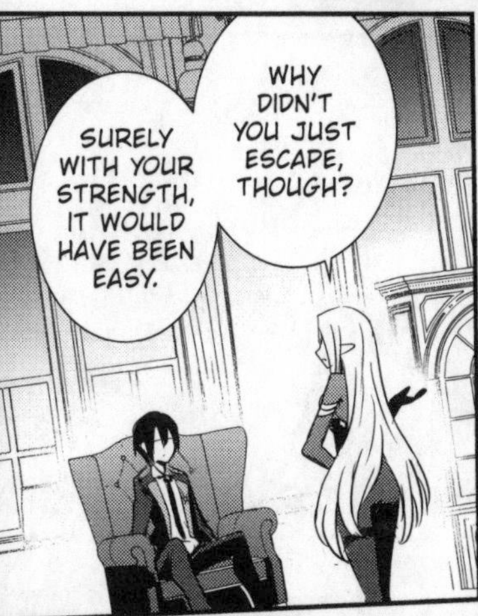

OF COURSE... THOUGH THAT DOESN'T EXPLAIN WHY YOU STARTED GOING OUT WITH THE PRINCESS TO BEGIN WITH.
I'M SURE YOU HAD SOME REASON YOU CAN'T TELL US.
I UNDER-STAND.
I KNOW YOU MUST BE CARRYING SOME TREMENDOUS BURDEN...
※ THERE'S NO BURDEN.
FOR NOW, FOCUS ON REGAIN-ING YOUR STRENGTH.
I IMAGINE YOU DON'T HAVE MUCH APPETITE AFTER THAT INTERROGA-TION...
...BUT YOU SHOULD TRY EATING THESE SLICED TUNA SANDWICHES ANYWAY.

HELL YEAH, I WAS STARVING.
WE DID SOME DIGGING ON OUR END.
THE KNIGHT ORDER IS PLANNING TO PIN THE CRIME ON YOU.

IT SEEMS SOME OF THEIR MEMBERS ARE WITH THE CULT OF DIABLOS.
AH, SO THAT'S THE WAY SHE WANTS TO SPIN IT.

THE KIDNAPPER MUST BE WITH THE CULT AS WELL.
I ASSUME THEY'RE AFTER ALEXIA'S BLOOD.
THEY PROBABLY PLAN ON USING IT SOMEHOW TO HELP RESURRECT THE DEMON.

IF THEY NEED HER BLOOD, THEY'LL BE KEEPING HER ALIVE.

THAT MEANS THERE'S STILL A CHANCE TO SAVE HER.

TH... THAT'S EXACTLY RIGHT.

I SHOULD HAVE KNOWN YOU'D FIGURED EVERYTHING OUT ALREADY ...!!

YOU MEAN DELTA THE SUICIDE WEAPON, THE HOTHEAD WHO PUT ALL HER POINTS INTO OFFENSE...?

THAT'S RIGHT. SHE'S BEEN DYING TO SEE YOU.

AND WITH THAT AS A DISTRACTION, WE'LL TRACK THE PRINCESS'S MAGIC AND RESCUE HER.

WE MOVE TOMOR-ROW.

WHEN WE'RE READY, I'LL SEND BETA OVER.

TO (LEAP)

ON THE WALL, A FAMOUS PAINTING I PICKED UP FROM A MERCHANT WAGON.

AN ANTIQUE LAMP TO LIGHT UP THE ROOM.

AH...

MY HEART IS SO FULL RIGHT NOW.

I HUNTED BANDITS NONSTOP.

I EVEN SCOOPED UP COINS ON MY HANDS AND KNEES.

NOW, THIS IS THE MOMENT...

...ALL THAT MONEY-GRUBBING WAS LEADING TO!!

THE NEXT DAY

MASTER SHADOW...

TO (TMP)

...ALL THE PREPARATIONS ARE COMPLETE.

THE TIME IS RIPE...
THE SHADOWS RUN THE WORLD TONIGHT...

DOKIIN (BADUMP)
ドキーン
THAT'S... PORDEAUX WINE...
A SINGLE BOTTLE CAN COST AS MUCH AS NINE HUNDRED THOUSAND ZENI...
THE LAMP IS ADORNED WITH JEWELS.
AND THAT PAINTING ...!!
ISN'T THAT A FAMOUS, PRICELESS MASTER-PIECE!!?
TO BE SO SOMBER DESPITE HAVING THE POWER TO AMASS ALL THESE TOP-CLASS ITEMS...
...IT MUST BE BECAUSE OF THE TREMENDOUS BURDEN HE CARRIES.
BURU
ブル
BURU (QUIVER)
ブル
※ THERE'S NO BURDEN.

...MASTER SHADOW.
ON ALPHA'S ORDERS, I'VE ASSEMBLED ALL AVAILABLE MEMBERS IN THE CAPITAL.
WE NUMBER 144 STRONG.
144!?
Y-YES, SIR!
IS THAT NOT ENOUGH!?
YOU HIRED EXTRAS...?
...EX-TRAS?
NOTHING, JUST TALKING TO MYSELF.
THE PLAN STARTS WITH DELTA'S SURPRISE ATTACK, WHICH WILL BE THE SIGNAL TO—
KA (THUNK)
...A LETTER...?
"IF YOU WANT ALEXIA BACK, COME TO THE WOODED PATH IN FRONT OF THE SCHOOL"...!?

MASTER SHADOW, IS THIS WHAT IT LOOKS LIKE!?

IT WAS DELIVERED HERE JUST YESTERDAY.

PROBABLY BY SOMEONE LOOKING TO FRAME ME.

MY APOLOGIES TO DELTA...

...BUT THIS PRELUDE...

...IS MINE TO PERFORM.

IS THAT...

...ALEXIA'S SHOE?

ZA (STEP)

HEY THERE, LOVER BOY.

WHATCHA DOING WITH THE PRINCESS'S SHOE?

OH, LOOK—THAT'S ALL THE PROOF WE NEED.

M-ME...!?
NO, THIS IS ALL A MISTAKE! SOMEONE JUST TOLD ME TO COME HERE...
WE CAUGHT YOU RED-HANDED. YOU'RE NOT TALKING YOUR WAY OUT OF THIS ONE.
BA (WSHH)
CID KAGE-NOU!!
YOU'RE UNDER ARREST FOR KID-NAPPING THE PRINCESS!!
IF YOU'D JUST FESSED UP FROM THE START...
...WE WOULDN'T HAVE HAD TO COME OUT TONIGHT.
GURA (STAGGER)

...HUH?

AHHHHHHH!! MY LEEEG!!

DOSU (SPLURT)

WH...

COME MORNING-ING...

...YOUR LIFE WILL BE FORFEIT!!

...PER-HAPS.

BUT IT MATTERS NOT.

MASTER SHADOW IS SO COOL...!

ZAKA (SCRIBBLE)

ZAKA

ZAKA

※ *BETA'S HANDWRITTEN* THE CHRONICLES OF MASTER SHADOW

FOR WHEN DAWN BREAKS...

...ALL OF THIS WILL BE OVER...
ZAN (SLASH)

DOOOO (KASHOOM)

IT SEEMS DELTA'S STARTED HER RAMPAGE.

LET'S GO, BETA.

SHUPA (ZOOM)

O-OF COURSE, MASTER SHADOW!!

THE NOCTURNE HAS BEGUN.

To be continued in *The Eminence in Shadow*, Vol. 2

The Eminence in Shadow

You're reading
the wrong way!
Flip to the back to read a
short story by the author of
THE Eminence IN Shadow
Daisuke Aizawa!

With the full moon outside the window illuminating me from behind, I give my longcoat a flourish.

"My name is Shadow. I lurk in the darkness and hunt down shadows..."

I can hear Beta audibly gulp.

In a building that looks like a laboratory, a man with slicked-back gray hair listens to a report from his subordinate.

"You're telling me we lost contact with our spy? He was always a bit of an odd one, but his skills were the real deal."

"Viscount Grease, we have to consider the possibility that information on the Cult of Diablos got leaked."

"We might be able to find out more by searching his last known location. Look into it now."

Upon receiving the order, his subordinate leaves.

"Just you wait, Millia. Once I find the heroes' blood, I'll finally be able to..."

Grease's voice echoes into the darkness.

and never found it."

The man with the drunken eyes looks up at me and shakes his head.

"Of course, there were some things I did find. I found magic, and that's how I got where I am now. So don't give up on hope, no matter how faint—though you should remember our days are numbered and everyone only gets so many. Even if you keep searching for something, there's no guarantee you'll find it."

"Dia...blos...exists..."

"Look, it's fine to keep believing. But you can't let yourself stop there. If something doesn't exist, you have to make it with your own two hands."

"What are you...talking about...?"

"The Cult of Diablos exists in my heart. And those feelings you have, those'll live on inside of me, too. So you can rest easy."

"Y-you're...you're crazy..."

"Crazy smart? Yeah, I know. Now, say good night."

I end the man's suffering. In his final moments, the drunkenness in his eyes vanishes, replaced with such clarity, he seems like a whole new person.

A little while later, Alpha and Beta return with cleaning supplies and slime.

"Did you get him to talk?"

"Yeah. Sure enough, he was an agent working for the Cult."

Alpha clenches her fist, and Beta leans forward in rapt attention.

"And I learned some important information. The Cult is making their move. Soon, the world will descend into darkness."

alcoholic.

Everyone in this world's heard the legend of Diablos the demon. But it's just a fairy tale, and the only ones who think it's actually real are kids and nutjobs.

"Revive…Diablos…"

As the man with the drunken eyes mumbles on, I start to feel sorry for him.

I know just how he feels. If things had played out a little differently, I might even have ended up like him.

"So you lost hope and abandoned yourself to the darkness…" I draw my slime sword.

"Be careful," Alpha warns me. "There's more to him than meets the eye."

"Yeah, I know."

Suddenly, with a *whoosh*, the man vanishes into the shadows.

And then—two swords meet.

I wipe away some blood. Behind me, the man with the drunken eyes collapses to the floor.

Alpha's eyes go wide. "That was so fast… I couldn't see a thing…"

The downed kidnapper is still breathing.

"I want to talk to him alone," I say.

"Of course, to force information out of him. I'll go get supplies to dispose of the body and the blood. Come on, Beta."

Beta trembles in fear as Alpha leads her out of the bedroom. The defeated man lets out a faint whisper. "Diablos…"

"You want to believe. I get it. I was the same as you once." I speak to him gently. "Back in my previous life, I searched everywhere for a mythical eight-headed serpent

"For now, I want to wait and observe him. It shouldn't be long before he acts."

"At long last, an actual battle against the Cult… If we promise not to get in your way, do you mind if we accompany you? We might not be of much help yet, but I think it'll be a good learning experience."

"…Very well."

And with that, Operation: Take Down the Kidnapper begins.

Moonlight streams into the bedroom as a lone figure quietly creeps across it.

When they get to the bed, they pull out something that looks like a rope and reach for the blankets—only to be met with a surprise.

"If you're looking for my sister, she's asleep in my room."

I grab the intruder's arm and send them flying.

"Gah…!"

I look at the figure frantically scrambling to his feet. It's a man in a dark cloak with a large, drooping hood—the sketchy guy from before. He must have been casing the joint when I caught his gaze in the afternoon.

"Don't even try running."

Alpha moves to block the door, and Beta peeks in from behind her. Realizing he's surrounded, the hooded man draws his sword.

"Dia…blos…"

Upon hearing the man's murmur, Alpha glares at him.

"I see. We weren't wrong about him being part of the Cult."

But I wasn't born yesterday. I can see it in his eyes. They're hollow and empty, like the eyes of a dead-drunk we'll need our organization to become larger and more powerful still."

"Oh yeah, fair enough."

I guess that tracks. Adding more people will add more problems, and it's not like I actually want a big organization. We are all just kids, though. What's the worst that could happen?

"And third, we've found someone who might be affiliated with the Cult. We spotted a suspicious character when we went into town to do reconnaissance, and then later, we saw him staring into Claire's room."

"Oh, that guy?"

"You already knew about him? I should have expected as much."

She must be talking about the weirdo I spotted when Claire and I were stretching. Of course, there's no way he's actually a member of the Cult of Diablos, since the Cult doesn't really exist and all.

I bet he's just some kidnapper who's after my sister. It makes sense seeing how she's got the hopes of the Kagenou family riding on her back, and kids of aristocrats get held for ransom all the time.

He could also just be some regular old burglar or robber, of course. But whatever he is, I welcome him with open arms. Whenever someone tries breaking into our house, I always make sure to give them a fitting reception.

"We suspect Claire caught his eye when she won the tournament. That was how the Cult of Diablos found out she was one of the possessed," Alpha adds.

"Precisely," I reply. "I tailed him after the tournament."

I did no such thing, obviously.

"To think you already went that far…"

"I haven't had bacon in ages!"

Alpha's face lights up. Normally, all I can get her is jerky.

"Beta, come on out. There's bacon!" Alpha calls over a silver-haired elf who she found the other day. Beta is the cabin's newest inhabitant.

I healed her since she was possessed, too, but she's pretty shy and seems a bit scared of me. Either that or she's afraid of humans in general.

Apparently, the two of them go way back, so I decided to leave Alpha in charge of taking care of her.

Beta keeps stealing glances at me as she lights up the stove and gets the frying pan ready.

"Today, I'm going to give you more intel on the Cult of Diablos. Then, we'll move on to drills to help you control your magic better."

I'm pretending to have performed another investigation. This "intel" is just an excuse to incorporate my newest plot devices to the Cult's backstory.

"Sounds good," Alpha replies. "But first, let's eat. Care to join us?"

"I'm good. I ate back at the house."

"I see. In that case, I have three reports to share with you. First, we're thinking of plowing a field behind the house. I feel bad for making you bring us food all the time, so I want us to be more self-sufficient."

"Cool. You'll need seeds and tools and stuff, so I'll make sure to get you some."

"Thank you. Second, now that Beta is joining me here, we want to expand the cabin. It won't be long before we need the facility to be larger."

"That's fine, but are you sure it's necessary?"

"It will be. If we're going up against the Cult of Diablos,

"Well, you've got the stretches to thank for that. Calves next."

"Fine. Let's just get this over with."

She gripes and moans, but she always goes along with it.

Meanwhile, I secretly continue her treatment by passing my magic through her body. In a few more days, I should be able to completely stabilize her.

"Your body's really loosened up. A few more days of this, and we can call it good on the stretching," I tell her.

"Wait, we're done already? B-but my glutes still feel so tight!"

"Oh, huh, looks like they are. That's weird; we loosened them just a minute ago."

"The stretches must go on, it seems."

The treatment will be done soon, but it looks like I'll keep having to stretch with her. I sigh in exasperation.

Suddenly, I sense someone watching me. I peer out the window.

"What's wrong?"

"Nothing." I resume stretching. It wasn't a big deal—just some creepy guy peeping through my sister's window.

That night, I slip out of the house once everyone else is asleep and head for the forest.

Deep in the woods, under the quiet moonlit branches, there's a small cabin. Alpha and I built it together.

"I brought food."

When I shout into the cabin, Alpha emerges. She's an elf with blue eyes and beautiful blond hair. Every day, I pilfer stuff from the kitchen and bring it here.

"Got you some eggs, bread, and potatoes. And check this out: I was able to get my hands on some bacon today."

The Eminence in Shadow

Special:

"I Searched Everywhere for a Mythical Eight-Headed Serpent and Never Found It"
By Daisuke Aizawa

Two months have passed since I turned that blob of flesh back into Alpha.

It's been a great two months—spent polishing up the backstories for the Shadow Garden and the Cult of Diablos and training my very first follower. I was well on my way to becoming a proper shadowbroker.

Then, one day, my sister becomes possessed.

She tries to hide it, but I can tell she's losing control of her magic like Alpha once did.

That's why I'm in the middle of surreptitiously healing her right now. My method of choice? Stretches.

"C'mon, Sis. Straighten your knee."

"I'm trying! You know, I really don't understand the point of all this."

I'm helping her deepen the stretch by pressing against her back. This is my excuse.

Curing the possession requires transferring your magic into the afflicted through touch. Plus, getting up close lets me check in on her condition, too.

"They say that when your body loosens up, your swordplay limbers up, too," I reply.

"Now that you mention it, I do remember having a longer range in that tournament I won the other day…"

That was because the possession was changing the quantity and density of her magic, but I'm not about to tell her that, obviously.

Art
Anri Sakano
Original Story
Daisuke Aizawa
Character Design
Touzai

THE Eminence IN Shadow 1

LETTERING: Phil Christie

TRANSLATION: Nathaniel Hiroshi Thrasher

Yen Press
150 West 30th Street
19th Floor
New York, NY 10001

Visit us at yenpress.com
facebook.com/yenpress
twitter.com/yenpress
yenpress.tumblr.com
instagram.com/yenpress

First Yen Press Edition: July 2021

Yen Press is an imprint of Yen Press, LLC.
The Yen Press name and logo are trademarks of Yen Press, LLC.

The publisher is not responsible for websites (or their content) that are not owned by the publisher.

Library of Congress Control Number: 2021935892

ISBNs: 978-1-9753-2518-3 (paperback)
978-1-9753-2519-0 (ebook)

10 9 8 7 6 5 4 3 2 1

BVG

Printed in the United States of America